Why there are leap years

The calendar is simply a system which has been invented by human beings to divide the passage of time into convenient units. The length of a day is obviously a unit of fundamental importance in human affairs and its length is largely determined by the rotation of the Earth about its axis. The second fundamental unit is the length of a year, which is the time it takes the Earth to complete its orbit around the Sun. It is this orbital motion which determines the changing of the seasons. It is very important to have a reliable calendar which matches the seasons and so indicates the best times to plant and harvest crops. By observation, it was found that the year is roughly $365\frac{1}{4}$ days long. The Julian calendar obtained this average over a cycle of four years. Three years of 365 days were followed by one leap year of 366 days, giving the average of $365\frac{1}{4}$ days. February 29th, the extra day, was added in those years which would divide by four. For instance, 1488 was a leap year but 1490 was not.

Since the Julian calendar was first introduced in 46 BC, it is interesting to speculate on how Caesar could have been able to get the future dates of leap years to divide by four. He could not have known either that Christ would be born or that sometime in the future, the whole world would base the starting point of its dates on the supposed year of his birth. Of course the present system of numbering the years did not come into widespread use until much later, in fact, not until Christianity became the official religion of the Roman Empire in the reign of Constantine. In 325 AD, there was a Council of Nicaea which determined the rule for calculating the date for Easter and it was probably from about then that the zero for the numbering system was fixed. Since the exact date of the birth of Christ was not known, the zero could well have been chosen so that the dates of leap years would divide by four. It certainly makes it easy to remember whether a year is a leap year or not.

Why the year starts on January 1st

Since the Earth orbits the Sun continuously, there is no obvious date to begin the year. In Ancient Egypt and Babylon, the year began at the autumn equinox, when day and night are equal in length. This is the day we call September 21st. The Ancient Greeks for a while chose the winter solstice, the shortest day of the year, which is the day we call December 21st. There is a certain logic to this date because it does seem rather like the dawn of a new year. It seems likely that Julius Caesar in reforming the Roman calendar also wanted to start the year from the winter solstice. However the Romans traditionally began the new year with a festival of the new moon. In the year of the change, the first new moon was about ten days after the winter solstice and that day became January 1st. The year 46 BC had 445 days to achieve this. As you might imagine, 46 BC became known as "The Year of Confusions". However all the trouble was worthwhile as the calendar which was then introduced lasted for more than 1600 years.

The start of the Civil or Legal Year in England

In medieval times in England, the start of the year was officially changed to March 25th, the date of the Annunciation. This is the date when the Church celebrates the announcement to Mary by the Archangel Gabriel that she is to bear the infant Jesus. During this intensely religious period of our history, it is easy to see why that date was chosen to represent a new beginning. However, gradually other countries settled for the Roman New Year's Day of January 1st and even in England some people did the same. Samuel Pepys describes a New Year's Eve Ball, attended by the King himself, which took place in 1662. It was held not on March 24th as one might expect, but on December 31st. The official date for the start of the new year was changed back to January 1st in 1752.

Why a week has 7 days

Since neither 365 nor 366 will divide exactly by 7, it is perhaps rather surprising that the week was chosen to be 7 days. At various times and in various parts of the world, the week has been fixed at between 5 and 10 days. The Romans chose 7 and this has gradually spread around the globe as it was felt to be "about right". For a long period, Sunday was a day of rest, and it seemed to suit human nature to have a rhythm of about 6 days of work and then a day of rest. To the Romans, 7 was a lucky number and they could also see 7 bright objects in the sky, which appeared to move against the background of the stars. Apart from the Sun and Moon, they could see five planets, Venus, Jupiter, Saturn, Mars and Mercury. They named the days of the week after these 7 "wanderers". The actual order of the days was based on astrology and was connected with the distance each was supposed to be from the Earth. The names of these celestial bodies and the gods associated with them have strongly influenced the names of the days in modern European languages.

CELESTIAL BODY	SAXON GOD	ENGLISH	FRENCH	GERMAN
Sun		Sunday	Dimanche	Sonntag
Moon		Monday	Lundi	Montag
Mars	Twi	Tuesday	Mardi	Dienstag
Mercury	Woden	Wednesday	Mercredi	Mittwoch
Jupiter	Thor	Thursday	Jeudi	Donnerstag
Venus	Friga	Friday	Vendredi	Freitag
Saturn		Saturday	Samedi	Samstag

The Saxon or Nordic equivalents of the Roman Gods have influenced English and German names but not the French. Thor was the god of thunder, and "Donner" in German means "thunder". If "Lundi" does not look like Moon, remember that the French word for "Moon" is "Lune". It is true that "Mittwoch" in German begins with "M" as does Mercury, but that is just a coincidence. Mittwoch means "middle of the week".

In Japan, which is a long way from Western Europe and subject to very different influences, the names of the days of the week still bear similarities. They are Sun-day, Moon-day, Fire-day, Water-day, Wood-day, Metal-day and Earth-day.

Days, Months & Years

A perpetual calendar
for the past, present and future

Magdalen Bear

TARQUIN PUBLICATIONS

Contents

The Story of the Calendar

4. Why the calendar differs year by year.
5. Why there are leap years.
6. Why a week has 7 days.
7. Why there are 12 months in a year.
7. How Easter is calculated.
8. The Julian Calendar sequence.
10. What went wrong with the Julian Calendar.
12. The changeover in Britain and America.
14. Adopting the New Style Calendar.
15. The Gregorian Calendar sequence.
16. Towards a better calendar.

The Calendars

21. The Monday Year
23. The Tuesday Year
25. The Wednesday Year
27. The Thursday Year
29. The Friday Year
31. The Saturday Year
33. The Sunday Year
35. The Monday Leap Year
37. The Tuesday Leap Year
39. The Wednesday Leap Year
41. The Thursday Leap Year
43. The Friday Leap Year
45. The Saturday Leap Year
47. The Sunday Leap Year

The Story of the Calendar

Why the calendar differs year by year

We know from experience that a calendar or diary from one year cannot be used again the following year. The pattern of days is different. Changing the calendar is as much a part of the New Year's celebrations as is making resolutions or singing "Auld Lang Syne!". Yet there is obviously a clear structure to the sequence of days and the purpose of this book is to explain it, so that we can find the correct calendar for any year, past, present or future.

Common sense tells us that the year can only start in one of seven different ways. New Year's Day, January 1st, has to fall on one day of the week and then the pattern of the calendar is fixed for the whole year. Each ordinary year which starts on a Monday must have the same sequence of days as any other ordinary year which starts on a Monday. Likewise, any leap year which starts on a Monday has to have the same sequence of days as any other leap year starting on a Monday. So there are seven different calendars for ordinary years and seven for leap years, fourteen in all. The complete set is printed at the end of this book and one can easily imagine that the manufacturers of calendars and diaries will keep all fourteen sets of printing plates in stock. All they have to do is to bring out the correct set for each new year.

The problem of choosing the correct calendar for any year is therefore simplified to that of finding on which day January 1st falls. An ordinary year of 365 days is 52 weeks and 1 day, whereas a leap year of 366 days is 52 weeks and 2 days. The day of January 1st must therefore move on by one day after an ordinary year and by two days afer a leap year. If New Year's Day happens to fall on a Thursday one year, then it must fall on either a Friday or a Saturday the following year, depending on whether it was or was not a leap year. In fact, that is where the name "leap year" comes from. After a leap year it "leaps" a day.

The Gregorian Calendar

Nowadays, all countries in the world use the "Gregorian" or "New Style" calendar which fixes which years are to be leap years, so determining the day of the week for January 1st for at least the next 3000 years. In Britain and America, this calendar was adopted in 1753 but some other countries have used it since 1583. It takes 400 years to complete the whole cycle and on page 15 there is the full chart. For any year after the new style calendar was introduced, all you have to do is to consult this chart to find which of the fourteen calendars applies.

The Julian Calendar

Until the relatively minor reforms which brought in the new style calendar, the one then in use was the "Julian" or "Old Style" calendar which was largely set up by Julius Caesar in 46 BC . The same set of fourteen yearly calendars was used but the cycle of the days of the week of January 1st was much simpler, taking only 28 years to complete. On page 8 there is a chart of that system and with a simple calculation you can find the correct calendar for any year whilst the Julian calendar was in use.

Why there are 12 months in a year

The word "month" is obviously connected with the word "moon" and its length is roughly that of a lunar month, the length of time between two full moons. A lunar month is $29\frac{1}{2}$ days, but a civil month can be 28,29,30 or 31 days. How this came about is largely due to a series of accidents of history. The early Romans had ten months in a year of probably only 304 days and the months were called after the words for first, second, third etc. With only 304 days the calendar quickly became out of step with the real year and so two extra months called Ianuarius and Februarius were added to the end of the year. Even with these additions, the calendar year was still too short and priests used to add extra days or months more or less whenever they wanted to.

Everything became very muddled and so the reforms introduced by Julius Caesar in 46 BC were very necessary. As part of these reforms the month Quintilis (meaning fifth, but now the seventh, because the beginning of the year had been moved to January 1st) was renamed Iulius after Caesar. The next emperor was Augustus Caesar and it was felt that so great a man should also have a month named after him. Sextilis (meaning sixth but by then the eighth) was renamed Augustus and given 31 days so that it would not be shorter than July. The extra day was taken from February.

By such reasons and events, the year has now been divided into 12 unequal months, seven of them having 31 days, 4 having 30 days and one having either 28 or 29. Any connection with lunar months has been abandoned, although the phases of the moon are still used to determine the dates of certain religious festivals like Ramadan or Easter.

How Easter is calculated

In the Christian calendar, Christmas is always on December 25th, but it can be on any day of the week. Easter Sunday, and other religious festivals like Good Friday or Ash Wednesday must be on the correct day of the week and therefore must change their dates from year to year. The ecclesiastical calendar for the whole year is based on the date of Easter, which itself is calculated from the date of the full moon. In the Western Church, Easter Sunday is the first Sunday after the first full moon on or after March 21st, the spring equinox. The full moon in this calculation is not quite the full moon you see in the sky, but a standardised full moon which evens out small differences and makes it possible to calculate the dates for years ahead. If the full moon falls on a Sunday, Easter Day is celebrated on the next Sunday. The earliest possible date for Easter Sunday is March 22nd (which last happened in 1818) and the latest possible date is April 25th (which last happened in 1943).

The dates for Easter Sunday until the year 2000 are			
1989	March 26th	1995	April 16th
1990	April 15th	1996	April 7th
1991	March 31st	1997	March 30th
1992	April 19th	1998	April 12th
1993	April 11th	1999	April 4th
1994	April 3rd	2000	April 23rd

The Julian Calendar sequence

REMAINDER AFTER DIVISION BY 28	DECIMAL REMAINDER	CALENDAR TO USE	REMAINDER AFTER DIVISION BY 28	DECIMAL REMAINDER	CALENDAR TO USE
0	.000	THURSDAY LEAP	14	.5	MONDAY
1	.035	SATURDAY	15	.535	TUESDAY
2	.071	SUNDAY	16	.571	WEDNESDAY LEAP
3	.107	MONDAY	17	.607	FRIDAY
4	.142	TUESDAY LEAP	18	.642	SATURDAY
5	.178	THURSDAY	19	.678	SUNDAY
6	.214	FRIDAY	20	.714	MONDAY LEAP
7	.25	SATURDAY	21	.75	WEDNESDAY
8	.285	SUNDAY LEAP	22	.785	THURSDAY
9	.321	TUESDAY	23	.821	FRIDAY
10	.357	WEDNESDAY	24	.857	SATURDAY LEAP
11	.392	THURSDAY	25	.892	MONDAY
12	.428	FRIDAY LEAP	26	.928	TUESDAY
13	.464	SUNDAY	27	.964	WEDNESDAY

Since there was a leap year every four years, the cycle of the days of the week of January 1st took 28 years to complete. To find the position of any particular year in the cycle, you have to divide the date by 28. Then use the remainder and this chart to find out which is the correct calendar for that year.

The remainder after the division appears as a whole number if you use the traditional "long division" method or as a decimal if you use a calculator. The number of times that 28 divides into the date does not matter. Only the remainder is important.

```
1 x 28 = 28    4 x 28 = 112    7 x 28 = 196
2 x 28 = 56    5 x 28 = 140    8 x 28 = 224
3 x 28 = 84    6 x 28 = 168    9 x 28 = 252
```

from 60.642857 use .642

If you are using "long division" then this part of the 28 times table will be useful.

If you are using a calculator then it will normally show many more decimal places than three. However, the first three digits after the decimal point will be sufficient to identify the correct calendar.

On the following pages are three examples of how the calculations are done, using both methods.

Find the correct yearly calendar for 1492

In 1492, the Julian Calendar was in use everywhere so we start by dividing 1492 by 28.

By long division

```
         53 r 8
28 ) 1492
     140
      92
      84
       8
```

By calculator

1492 ÷ 28
= 53.285

The digits after the decimal points are .285

Looking at the chart opposite, we see that either the remainder 8 or the digits after the decimal point .285 tell us that we should use the "Sunday Leap Year" calendar for the year 1492.

We can then see the calendar for the year when Columbus left to search for the Indies and discovered the New World. He set sail on August 3rd 1492, a Friday. On October 11th, a Thursday, they saw a branch floating in the sea which had fresh berries on it. The next day, Friday October 12th they sighted the land of the Americas for the first time.

Find the correct yearly calendar for 1666 in England

In England in 1666, the Julian Calendar was in use, so we start by dividing 1666 by 28.

By long division

```
         59 r 14
28 ) 1666
     140
     266
     252
      14
```

By calculator

1666 ÷ 28
= 59.5
The digit after the decimal point is .5

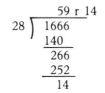

Looking at the chart opposite, we see that either the remainder 14 or the digit after the decimal point .5 tells us that we should use the "Monday Year" calendar for the year 1666.

We can then see the calendar for the year when the Great Fire of London took place. It was first discovered early in the morning of September 2nd, a Sunday, in Pudding Lane. At first it burned slowly, but fanned by a north-easterly wind grew and grew in strength. On Monday September 3rd London Bridge was burning and by Wednesday September 5th most of the city had been burned to the ground, including St Paul's Cathedral. The diary of Samuel Pepys is a most interesting way to read about this terrible event written by someone who was actually there.

Find the correct yearly calendar for 1522

In 1522, the Julian Calendar was in use everywhere, so we start by dividing 1522 by 28.

By long division

$$\begin{array}{r} 54 \text{ r } 10 \\ 28 \overline{) 1522} \\ \underline{140} \\ 122 \\ \underline{112} \\ 10 \end{array}$$

By calculator

$1522 \div 28$
$= 54.357$

The digits after the decimal points are .357

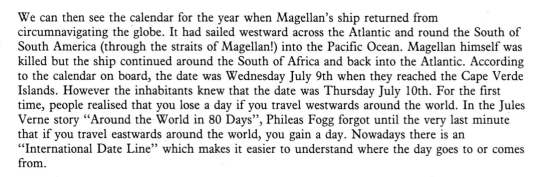

Consulting the chart on page 8, we see that either the remainder 10 or the digits after the decimal point .357 tell us that we should use the "Wednesday Year" calendar for the year 1522.

We can then see the calendar for the year when Magellan's ship returned from circumnavigating the globe. It had sailed westward across the Atlantic and round the South of South America (through the straits of Magellan!) into the Pacific Ocean. Magellan himself was killed but the ship continued around the South of Africa and back into the Atlantic. According to the calendar on board, the date was Wednesday July 9th when they reached the Cape Verde Islands. However the inhabitants knew that the date was Thursday July 10th. For the first time, people realised that you lose a day if you travel westwards around the world. In the Jules Verne story "Around the World in 80 Days", Phileas Fogg forgot until the very last minute that if you travel eastwards around the world, you gain a day. Nowadays there is an "International Date Line" which makes it easier to understand where the day goes to or comes from.

What went wrong with the Julian Calendar

When the Julian calendar was set up, with the length of the year at $365 \frac{1}{4}$ days on average, it was expected that it would keep in step with astronomical reality for ever. This proved not to be the case, as the length of the year is not $365 \frac{1}{4}$ days exactly, but is 11 minutes and 14 seconds shorter. This does not sound very much, but it amounts to one whole day every 128 years. The spring equinox had been set to March 21st in 325 AD, but as the centuries passed the date of the equinox became earlier and earlier. In the year 1580 AD it was on March 11th. Since the spring equinox was used to calculate the date of Easter and it was drifting back towards Christmas, something had to be done. The difference was by then 10 days and the Pope, Gregory X111, advised by the astronomer Clavius, decreed that 10 days should be removed from 1582. Thursday October 4th 1582 should be followed by Friday October 15th. This was accepted by most Catholic countries, but was ignored by most Protestant countries and by the Eastern Church.

How the error was corrected

Although the accumulated 10 day error had been corrected by the sudden adjustment, this was not sufficient to solve the problem forever. A new error would begin to build up again year by year. The problem was that the Julian Calendar gives three leap years too many in each period of roughly four centuries. The solution was a very simple one. Under the "New Style" or "Gregorian" calendar, the century years would not be treated as leap years unless the date itself divided by four hundred. Under this rule, the years 1700, 1800 and 1900 should not be leap years. Although they do divide exactly by four, they do not divide by four hundred. The years 1600 and 2000 should be leap years. Of course this new calendar is not exactly correct either, but it will be another 3000 years before a further correction is needed.

October							November						
M	Tu	W	Th	F	Sa	Su	M	Tu	W	Th	F	Sa	Su
1	2	3	4	15	16	17	1	2	3	4	5	6	7
18	19	20	21	22	23	24	8	9	10	11	12	13	14
25	26	27	28	29	30	31	15	16	17	18	19	20	21
							22	23	24	25	26	27	28
							29	30					

October and November 1582 in those countries which adopted the new style Calendar.

October							November						
M	Tu	W	Th	F	Sa	Su	M	Tu	W	Th	F	Sa	Su
1	2	3	4	5	6	7					1	2	3	4
8	9	10	11	12	13	14	5	6	7	8	9	10	11
15	16	17	18	19	20	21	12	13	14	15	16	17	18
22	23	24	25	26	27	28	19	20	21	22	23	24	25
29	30	31					26	27	28	29	30		

October and November 1582 in those countries which did not change.

Those countries which accepted the 10 day change also accepted the new scheme of leap years. Until 1700 there was a difference of 10 days between the date observed in some countries and that in others. For instance, the first Sunday in October 1582 was called October 17th or October 7th, depending on where you lived. The year 1700 was treated as a leap year under the old system, but not under the new and so the difference then became 11 days. In Britain, it was additionally confusing because although the Civil or Legal Year began on March 25th, many people continued to use the Roman Year beginning on January 1st. For dates between January 1st and March 24th there was doubt about which year was really meant and so it became customary to mark documents in a double form. For instance, the date might be given as February 17th 1626-27. This indicated that the January 1st people considered it to be 1627 and the March 25th people considered it to be 1626.

The calendars in this book and the method of calculating the correct Julian Calendar to use are consistently of the "historical" variety, starting on January 1st and ending on December 31st. If you want to look at the civil calendar for say 1626, then you need to use two different ones for the two parts of the year. The period from March 25th to December 31st is on the "Sunday Year" calendar (1626 divided by 28 leaves remainder 2). The period from January 1st – March 24th falls into the historical year of 1627. Hence you should use the "Monday Year" calendar for that part of the year (1627 divided by 28 leaves remainder 3).

The changeover in Britain and America

It was finally decided to introduce the Gregorian Calendar into Britain and also to bring New Year's Day to January 1st during the civil years of 1751 and 1752.

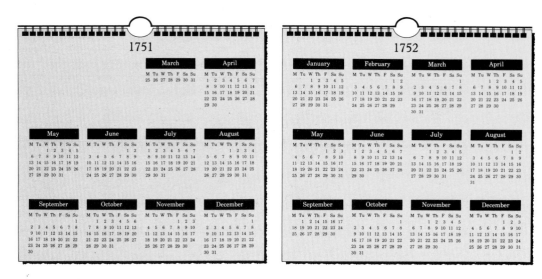

The year 1751 began as usual on March 25th, but ended on December 31st, having lost 84 days. In 1752, Wednesday September 2nd was followed by Thursday September 14th. Although the changes were carefully announced and special arrangements were made so that people did not have to pay rent for the missing days, many people felt that somehow they had been cheated out of some of their lives. There were even reports of riots in the streets in September 1752 with people shouting "Give us back our 11 days".

September

M	Tu	W	Th	F	Sa	Su
	1	2	14	15	16	17
18	19	20	21	22	23	24
25	26	27	28	29	30	

September

M	Tu	W	Th	F	Sa	Su
				1	2	3
4	5	6	7	8	9	10
11	12	13	14	15	16	17
18	19	20	21	22	23	24
25	26	27	28	29	30	

September 1752 in Britain and America.

September 1752 in those countries using the Gregorian Calendar.

From Thursday September 14th 1752, the calendars were once again in step.

The need for standardised dating

If we read an original document today we must bear in mind the dating system which the writer used. For instance, a letter dated March 25th 1711 was written 364 days before one dated March 24th 1711, at least if the writer lived in England or in the American Colonies. Someone living in France and dating a letter March 25th 1711 was writing the day after one dated March 24th 1711, because on the Continent the year began on January 1st. Ambassadors, writing between one country and another, dated their letters according to the system in use in the country where they were based.

Because of the possibility of confusion, historians often choose to change dates on documents to a standardised Gregorian form. For instance, if you look in an encyclopaedia or history book, it will say that George Washington was born on February 22nd 1732. However, if there had been a calendar in the room at the time, it would have said "February 11th 1731", because at the time the English Colonies still used the Julian Calendar with the official year beginning on March 25th. Changing the year to the historical year beginning on January 1st, brought his birthday into 1732 and the dropping of 11 days when he was 20 brought his standardised birthday to February 22nd 1732. If this seems a strange thing to do, realize that if a French surgeon had attended the birth, he might have recorded the date on the certificate as February 22nd 1732.

This diagram shows the relationship between the various years.

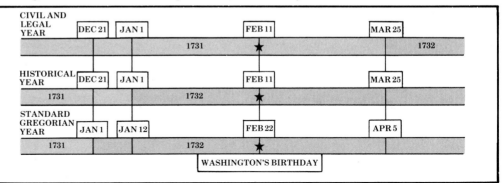

The Tax Year in Britain

There is another consequence of the calendar changes, which can be seen even today. Taxes are not collected for the year from January 1st to December 31st, but from April 6th one year to April 5th the next. This came about in the following manner. Traditionally, taxes were collected for the year on the first day of the following year. Until 1751, that was on March 25th. It was obviously unfair to collect a whole year's taxes on a year that was 84 days short and so the taxes for 1751 were collected on March 25th 1752. The year of 1752 was 11 days short and so taxes were not collected on March 25th 1753, but 11 days later on April 5th. This would be the date still in use, except for the fact that these changes were not at first totally accepted. The year 1800 should not have been a leap year, but in financial circles it was treated as one. The first day of the tax year then had to be corrected by one further day to April 6th during the nineteenth century. It has remained on this date to the present day.

Adopting the New Style Calendar

Gradually all the countries of the world have adopted the Gregorian calendar, adjusting by 10, 11, 12 or 13 days depending on when the change was made. For a long period the date in some countries could differ from that in others. It is a curious fact that the famous "October Revolution", which took place in the Soviet Union in October 1917 according to the Russian Calendar, took place in November 1917 according to the calendar used by most other countries. The changeover was not made until after the revolution.

Also, all countries have now adopted an official year beginning on January 1st. Certain societies, the Chinese for example, have retained their colourful traditional ceremonies to mark their own traditional New Year, but for all official purposes they use the same calendar as everyone else.

DATES FROM WHICH THE NEW-STYLE CALENDAR WAS USED

From 1583	Most of Western Europe
1587	Poland
1588	Hungary
1700	Denmark and the protestant states of Germany and Holland
1741	Sweden, which achieved the changeover gradually leaving out 11 leap years from 1700-1740
1753	Great Britain and the American Colonies
1873	Japan
1913	China
1916	Bulgaria
1919	Russia and Turkey
1920	Yugoslavia and Roumania
1924	Greece and the Eastern Church

The year 2000 is a leap year under both systems and so the difference would not have reached 14 days until March 1st 2100. However, there are now no countries which have not adopted the Gregorian Calendar.

The Gregorian Calendar Sequence

The complete cycle of the days on which January 1st occurs, showing which of the 14 calendars to use, repeats itself every 400 years. This chart is valid for any year up to 5000 AD, but for any particular country you have to be careful only to use it for dates after the changeover took place.

1600-1699 : 2000-2099 and every 400 years

Decades \ Years	0	1	2	3	4	5	6	7	8	9
0	Sa•	M	Tu•	W	Th•	Sa	Su	M	Tu•	Th
1	F	Sa	Su•	Tu	W	Th	F•	Su	M	Tu
2	W•	F	Sa	Su	M•	W	Th	F	Sa•	M
3	Tu	W	Th•	Sa	Su	M	Tu•	Th	F	Sa
4	Su•	Tu	W	Th	F•	Su	M	Tu	W•	F
5	Sa	Su	M•	W	Th	F	Sa•	M	Tu	W
6	Th•	Sa	Su	M	Tu•	Th	F	Sa	Su•	Tu
7	W	Th	F•	Su	M	Tu	W•	F	Sa	Su
8	M•	W	Th	F	Sa•	M	Tu	W	Th•	Sa
9	Su	M	Tu•	Th	F	Sa	Su•	Tu	W	Th

1700-1799 : 2100-2199 and every 400 years

Decades \ Years	0	1	2	3	4	5	6	7	8	9
0	F	Sa	Su	M	Tu•	Th	F	Sa	Su•	Tu
1	W	Th	F•	Su	M	Tu	W•	F	Sa	Su
2	M•	W	Th	F	Sa•	M	Tu	W	Th•	Sa
3	Su	M	Tu•	Th	F	Sa	Su•	Tu	W	Th
4	F•	Su	M	Tu	W•	F	Sa	Su	M•	W
5	Th	F	Sa•	M	Tu	W	Th•	Sa	Su	M
6	Tu•	Th	F	Sa	Su•	Tu	W	Th	F•	Su
7	M	Tu	W•	F	Sa	Su	M•	W	Th	F
8	Sa•	M	Tu	W	Th•	Sa	Su	M	Tu•	Th
9	F	Sa	Su•	Tu	W	Th	F•	Su	M	Tu

1800-1899 : 2200-2299 and every 400 years

Decades \ Years	0	1	2	3	4	5	6	7	8	9
0	W	Th	F	Sa	Su•	Tu	W	Th	F•	Su
1	M	Tu	W•	F	Sa	Su	M•	W	Th	F
2	Sa•	M	Tu	W	Th•	Sa	Su	M	Tu•	Th
3	F	Sa	Su•	Tu	W	Th	F•	Su	M	Tu
4	W•	F	Sa	Su	M•	W	Th	F	Sa•	M
5	Tu	W	Th•	Sa	Su	M	Tu•	Th	F	Sa
6	Su•	Tu	W	Th	F•	Su	M	Tu	W•	F
7	Sa	Su	M•	W	Th	F	Sa•	M	Tu	W
8	Th•	Sa	Su	M	Tu•	Th	F	Sa	Su•	Tu
9	W	Th	F•	Su	M	Tu	W•	F	Sa	Su

1900-1999 : 2300-2399 and every 400 years

Decades \ Years	0	1	2	3	4	5	6	7	8	9
0	M	Tu	W	Th	F•	Su	M	Tu	W•	F
1	Sa	Su	M•	W	Th	F	Sa•	M	Tu	W
2	Th•	Sa	Su	M	Tu•	Th	F	Sa	Su•	Tu
3	W	Th	F•	Su	M	Tu	W•	F	Sa	Su
4	M•	W	Th	F	Sa•	M	Tu	W	Th•	Sa
5	Su	M	Tu•	Th	F	Sa	Su•	Tu	W	Th
6	F•	Su	M	Tu	W•	F	Sa	Su	M•	W
7	Th	F	Sa•	M	Tu	W	Th•	Sa	Su	M
8	Tu•	Th	F	Sa	Su•	Tu	W	Th	F•	Su
9	M	Tu	W•	F	Sa	Su	M•	W	Th	F

• The years marked with a dot are leap years.

Find which day of the week May 5th 1782 fell on

The year 1782 lies within the period 1700-1799. It is the second year of the eighth decade. The correct calendar to use is "The Tuesday Year".

							Years				
		0	1	2	3	4	5	6	7	8	9
	0	F	Sa	Su	M	Tu	Th	F	Sa	Su	Tu
	1	W	Th	F	Su	M	Tu	W	F	Sa	Su
	2	M	W	Th	F	Sa	M	Tu	W	Th	Sa
	3	Su	M	Tu	Th	F	Sa	Su	Tu	W	Th
Decades	4	F	Su	M	Tu	W	F	Sa	Su	M	W
	5	Th	F	Sa	M	Tu	W	Th	Sa	Su	M
	6	Tu	Th	F	Sa	Su	Tu	W	Th	F	Su
	7	M	Tu	W	F	Sa	Su	M	W	Th	F
	8	Sa	M	Tu	W	Th	Sa	Su	M	Tu	Th
	9	F	Sa	Su	Tu	W	Th	F	Su	M	Tu

1700-1799 : 2100-2199 and every 400 years

We can see that May 5th 1782 was a Sunday. The same chart shows that May 5th 2182, May 5th 2582, May 5th 2982 and so on, will also be Sundays.

Towards a better calendar

The present Gregorian Calendar, which is in use throughout the world, does keep the year in good balance with the realities of astronomy. However, it does appear to be unnecessarily complicated with months of different lengths occurring in different patterns throughout the year. It requires 14 different calendars and a cycle which lasts 400 years to deal with the complete sequence of possible years.

Also, when it comes to keeping national and international statistics, the different lengths of the months and the changing patterns of week-ends, makes it very difficult to compare one year with another. Perhaps a month of 30 or 31 days will have 4 Sundays, perhaps it will have 5. In years like 1976 and 2004, even February has 5 Sundays. In one year March might have 23 working days. The following year it might have 17. March and April are especially variable because Easter sometimes falls into one month and sometimes into the other.

Many people have proposed a reformed or improved calendar and it is interesting to think how it might be done on a more rational and scientific basis. Here are two possibilities.

Thirteen equal months in a year

January

Su	M	Tu	W	Th	F	Sa
1	2	3	4	5	6	7
8	9	10	11	12	13	14
15	16	17	18	19	20	21
22	23	24	25	26	27	28

February

Su	M	Tu	W	Th	F	Sa
1	2	3	4	5	6	7
8	9	10	11	12	13	14
15	16	17	18	19	20	21
22	23	24	25	26	27	28

March

Su	M	Tu	W	Th	F	Sa
1	2	3	4	5	6	7
8	9	10	11	12	13	14
15	16	17	18	19	20	21
22	23	24	25	26	27	28

April

Su	M	Tu	W	Th	F	Sa
1	2	3	4	5	6	7
8	9	10	11	12	13	14
15	16	17	18	19	20	21
22	23	24	25	26	27	28

May

Su	M	Tu	W	Th	F	Sa
1	2	3	4	5	6	7
8	9	10	11	12	13	14
15	16	17	18	19	20	21
22	23	24	25	26	27	28

June

Su	M	Tu	W	Th	F	Sa
1	2	3	4	5	6	7
8	9	10	11	12	13	14
15	16	17	18	19	20	21
22	23	24	25	26	27	28

Sol

Su	M	Tu	W	Th	F	Sa
1	2	3	4	5	6	7
8	9	10	11	12	13	14
15	16	17	18	19	20	21
22	23	24	25	26	27	28

L Leap Day

July

Su	M	Tu	W	Th	F	Sa
1	2	3	4	5	6	7
8	9	10	11	12	13	14
15	16	17	18	19	20	21
22	23	24	25	26	27	28

August

Su	M	Tu	W	Th	F	Sa
1	2	3	4	5	6	7
8	9	10	11	12	13	14
15	16	17	18	19	20	21
22	23	24	25	26	27	28

September

Su	M	Tu	W	Th	F	Sa
1	2	3	4	5	6	7
8	9	10	11	12	13	14
15	16	17	18	19	20	21
22	23	24	25	26	27	28

October

Su	M	Tu	W	Th	F	Sa
1	2	3	4	5	6	7
8	9	10	11	12	13	14
15	16	17	18	19	20	21
22	23	24	25	26	27	28

November

Su	M	Tu	W	Th	F	Sa
1	2	3	4	5	6	7
8	9	10	11	12	13	14
15	16	17	18	19	20	21
22	23	24	25	26	27	28

December

Su	M	Tu	W	Th	F	Sa
1	2	3	4	5	6	7
8	9	10	11	12	13	14
15	16	17	18	19	20	21
22	23	24	25	26	27	28

Y Year-End Day

The "Sol Calendar" is one such proposal. There would be an extra month called Sol which would be inserted between June and July. Every month would have 28 days and would begin on a Sunday. These 13 months would give 364 days and so the year would be one day short in an ordinary year and two days short in a leap year. The proposal is that there should be a "Year-End Day" or "Y" which falls after December 28th and before January 1st. It would not have a day of the week or belong to a month and would surely be a world-wide holiday to celebrate the end of one year and the beginning of the next. During leap years, an extra day called "Leap Day" or "L" would be inserted between Sol and July. It also would not have a day of the week or belong to a month and would surely also be a world-wide holiday, once every four years.

If this calendar was adopted, then it would have the disadvantage that there are no natural quarter years or half years because 13 has no smaller divisions. Some people would not like it because Friday 13th. would occur 13 times every year! Christmas Day would always be on a Wednesday and anyone born on a Friday would find that their birthday was always on a Friday. No fewer than 94 days would have to change month. It is interesting to construct a chart showing what the new Sol date would be for all the days of the present calendar.

Four equal quarters in a year

The "World Calendar"

January						
Su	M	Tu	W	Th	F	Sa
1	2	3	4	5	6	7
8	9	10	11	12	13	14
15	16	17	18	19	20	21
22	23	24	25	26	27	28
29	30	31				

February						
Su	M	Tu	W	Th	F	Sa
				1	2	3	4
5	6	7	8	9	10	11
12	13	14	15	16	17	18
19	20	21	22	23	24	25
26	27	28	29	30		

March						
Su	M	Tu	W	Th	F	Sa
					1	2
3	4	5	6	7	8	9
10	11	12	13	14	15	16
17	18	19	20	21	22	23
24	25	26	27	28	29	30

April						
Su	M	Tu	W	Th	F	Sa
1	2	3	4	5	6	7
8	9	10	11	12	13	14
15	16	17	18	19	20	21
22	23	24	25	26	27	28
29	30	31				

May						
Su	M	Tu	W	Th	F	Sa
				1	2	3	4
5	6	7	8	9	10	11
12	13	14	15	16	17	18
19	20	21	22	23	24	25
26	27	28	29	30		

June						
Su	M	Tu	W	Th	F	Sa
					1	2
3	4	5	6	7	8	9
10	11	12	13	14	15	16
17	18	19	20	21	22	23
24	25	26	27	28	29	30 L

July						
Su	M	Tu	W	Th	F	Sa
1	2	3	4	5	6	7
8	9	10	11	12	13	14
15	16	17	18	19	20	21
22	23	24	25	26	27	28
29	30	31				

August						
Su	M	Tu	W	Th	F	Sa
				1	2	3	4
5	6	7	8	9	10	11
12	13	14	15	16	17	18
19	20	21	22	23	24	25
26	27	28	29	30		

September						
Su	M	Tu	W	Th	F	Sa
					1	2
3	4	5	6	7	8	9
10	11	12	13	14	15	16
17	18	19	20	21	22	23
24	25	26	27	28	29	30

October						
Su	M	Tu	W	Th	F	Sa
1	2	3	4	5	6	7
8	9	10	11	12	13	14
15	16	17	18	19	20	21
22	23	24	25	26	27	28
29	30	31				

November						
Su	M	Tu	W	Th	F	Sa
				1	2	3	4
5	6	7	8	9	10	11
12	13	14	15	16	17	18
19	20	21	22	23	24	25
26	27	28	29	30		

December						
Su	M	Tu	W	Th	F	Sa
					1	2
3	4	5	6	7	8	9
10	11	12	13	14	15	16
17	18	19	20	21	22	23
24	25	26	27	28	29	30 Y

The "World Calendar" is another proposal which overcomes some of the disadvantages of the Sol Calendar, while retaining some of its features. There would be 12 months, as today, so there would be no need to introduce a new one. However, only January, April, July, and October would have 31 days. All the others would have 30 and each quarter would have a fixed pattern of one 31 day month followed by two 30 day months. This would give 364 days during the year. The extra day which is needed in an ordinary year would be the "Year-End Day" or "Y". As for the Sol Calendar, this would be inserted between December and January. The extra day "L" for a leap year would be inserted between June and July. Neither of these days would have a day of the week or belong to a month. Perhaps in future, babies who were born on these two special days would be thought to be especially lucky or honoured, just as today it is special to be born on Christmas Day or New Year's Day. It is also special nowadays to be born on February 29th, but many children born on that day do not consider it lucky as they have to wait four years (and occasionally eight) for their birthdays to come again.

This system has the advantage that all four quarters are exactly the same length, and that the calendar above is the only one that would be needed. Only 8 days would have to change from one month to another. This scheme is realistic and it was presented to the United Nations in 1956. However, it did not receive any votes as it was felt that the United Nations had more important things to do! Perhaps one day in the future, a new, more rational and scientific calendar will indeed be introduced, thus completing the work set in motion by Julius Caesar more than 2000 years ago.

The Calendars

For dates between 1900 and 1999 under the Gregorian Calendar use the chart below to find out which calendar to use.

	Years									
Decades	0	1	2	3	4	5	6	7	8	9
0	M	Tu	W	Th	F•	Su	M	Tu	W•	F
1	Sa	Su	M•	W	Th	F	Sa•	M	Tu	W
2	Th•	Sa	Su	M	Tu•	Th	F	Sa	Su•	Tu
3	W	Th	F•	Su	M	Tu	W•	F	Sa	Su
4	M•	W	Th	F	Sa•	M	Tu	W	Th•	Sa
5	Su	M	Tu•	Th	F	Sa	Su•	Tu	W	Th
6	F•	Su	M	Tu	W•	F	Sa	Su	M•	W
7	Th	F	Sa•	M	Tu	W	Th•	Sa	Su	M
8	Tu•	Th	F	Sa	Su•	Tu	W	Th	F•	Su
9	M	Tu	W•	F	Sa	Su	M•	W	Th	F

For all other New Style Gregorian Calendar dates see page 15.

For all Old Style Julian Calendar dates see page 8.

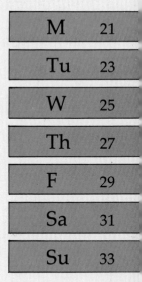

ORDINARY YEARS

M	21
Tu	23
W	25
Th	27
F	29
Sa	31
Su	33

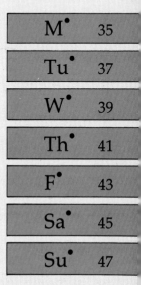

LEAP YEARS

M•	35
Tu•	37
W•	39
Th•	41
F•	43
Sa•	45
Su•	47

Monday Years Since 1753

1753 – 1799	1800 – 1899	1900 – 1999	2000 – 2099
1753	1810	1900	2001
1759	1821	1906	2007
1770	1827	1917	2018
1781	1838	1923	2029
1787	1849	1934	2035
1798	1855	1945	2046
	1866	1951	2057
	1877	1962	2063
	1883	1973	2074
	1894	1979	2085
		1990	2091

It was a Monday year when on . . . .

25th January 1759 Robert Burns, the Scottish poet, was born.

19th October 1781 The American War of Independence ended.

26th March 1827 Ludwig van Beethoven, the German composer, died.

28th June 1838 Queen Victoria was crowned.

4th July 1883 The Statue of Liberty was presented to the U.S.A. by France.

21st May 1894 The Manchester Ship Canal was officially opened.

23rd October 1906 Paul Cézanne, the French artist, died.

31st December 1923 The chimes of Big Ben were first used in a broadcast.

4th July 1934 Marie Curie, the scientist who discovered X-rays, died.

15th May 1979 A.A. Milne's son, the original Christopher Robin, opened the Pooh Sticks Bridge at Hartfield in Sussex.

The Monday Year

January

M	Tu	W	Th	F	Sa	Su
1	2	3	4	5	6	7
8	9	10	11	12	13	14
15	16	17	18	19	20	21
22	23	24	25	26	27	28
29	30	31				

February

M	Tu	W	Th	F	Sa	Su
			1	2	3	4
5	6	7	8	9	10	11
12	13	14	15	16	17	18
19	20	21	22	23	24	25
26	27	28				

March

M	Tu	W	Th	F	Sa	Su
			1	2	3	4
5	6	7	8	9	10	11
12	13	14	15	16	17	18
19	20	21	22	23	24	25
26	27	28	29	30	31	

April

M	Tu	W	Th	F	Sa	Su
						1
2	3	4	5	6	7	8
9	10	11	12	13	14	15
16	17	18	19	20	21	22
23	24	25	26	27	28	29
30						

May

M	Tu	W	Th	F	Sa	Su
	1	2	3	4	5	6
7	8	9	10	11	12	13
14	15	16	17	18	19	20
21	22	23	24	25	26	27
28	29	30	31			

June

M	Tu	W	Th	F	Sa	Su
				1	2	3
4	5	6	7	8	9	10
11	12	13	14	15	16	17
18	19	20	21	22	23	24
25	26	27	28	29	30	

July

M	Tu	W	Th	F	Sa	Su
						1
2	3	4	5	6	7	8
9	10	11	12	13	14	15
16	17	18	19	20	21	22
23	24	25	26	27	28	29
30	31					

August

M	Tu	W	Th	F	Sa	Su
	1	2	3	4	5	
6	7	8	9	10	11	12
13	14	15	16	17	18	19
20	21	22	23	24	25	26
27	28	29	30	31		

September

M	Tu	W	Th	F	Sa	Su
					1	2
3	4	5	6	7	8	9
10	11	12	13	14	15	16
17	18	19	20	21	22	23
24	25	26	27	28	29	30

October

M	Tu	W	Th	F	Sa	Su
1	2	3	4	5	6	7
8	9	10	11	12	13	14
15	16	17	18	19	20	21
22	23	24	25	26	27	28
29	30	31				

November

M	Tu	W	Th	F	Sa	Su
		1	2	3	4	
5	6	7	8	9	10	11
12	13	14	15	16	17	18
19	20	21	22	23	24	25
26	27	28	29	30		

December

M	Tu	W	Th	F	Sa	Su
					1	2
3	4	5	6	7	8	9
10	11	12	13	14	15	16
17	18	19	20	21	22	23
24	25	26	27	28	29	30
31						

Tuesday Years Since 1753

1753 – 1799	1800 – 1899	1900 – 1999	2000 – 2099
1754	1805	1901	2002
1765	1811	1907	2013
1771	1822	1918	2019
1782	1833	1929	2030
1793	1839	1935	2041
1799	1850	1946	2047
	1861	1957	2058
	1867	1963	2069
	1878	1974	2075
	1889	1985	2086
	1895	1991	2097

It was a Tuesday year when on . . . .

15th August 1771 Walter Scott, the Scottish novelist, was born.
21st October 1805 Horatio Lord Nelson was killed at the battle of Trafalgar.
30th October 1822 The Caledonian canal in Scotland was opened.
21st October 1833 Alfred Nobel, the Swedish industrialist and founder of the Nobel prize, was born.
16th April 1889 Charlie Chaplin, the film actor, was born.
22nd January 1901 Queen Victoria died.
16th July 1918 The last Tsar of all the Russias, Nicholas $\overline{\text{II}}$, was assassinated along with his family at Ekaterinburg.
22nd October 1946 The United Nations General Assembly met for the first time in New York.
4th October 1957 The first satellite was launched into space by the Russians.
22nd November 1963 John F. Kennedy, the U.S.A. President, was assassinated.

The Tuesday Year

January

M	Tu	W	Th	F	Sa	Su
	1	2	3	4	5	6
7	8	9	10	11	12	13
14	15	16	17	18	19	20
21	22	23	24	25	26	27
28	29	30	31			

February

M	Tu	W	Th	F	Sa	Su
				1	2	3
4	5	6	7	8	9	10
11	12	13	14	15	16	17
18	19	20	21	22	23	24
25	26	27	28			

March

M	Tu	W	Th	F	Sa	Su
				1	2	3
4	5	6	7	8	9	10
11	12	13	14	15	16	17
18	19	20	21	22	23	24
25	26	27	28	29	30	31

April

M	Tu	W	Th	F	Sa	Su
1	2	3	4	5	6	7
8	9	10	11	12	13	14
15	16	17	18	19	20	21
22	23	24	25	26	27	28
29	30					

May

M	Tu	W	Th	F	Sa	Su
		1	2	3	4	5
6	7	8	9	10	11	12
13	14	15	16	17	18	19
20	21	22	23	24	25	26
27	28	29	30	31		

June

M	Tu	W	Th	F	Sa	Su
					1	2
3	4	5	6	7	8	9
10	11	12	13	14	15	16
17	18	19	20	21	22	23
24	25	26	27	28	29	30

July

M	Tu	W	Th	F	Sa	Su
1	2	3	4	5	6	7
8	9	10	11	12	13	14
15	16	17	18	19	20	21
22	23	24	25	26	27	28
29	30	31				

August

M	Tu	W	Th	F	Sa	Su
			1	2	3	4
5	6	7	8	9	10	11
12	13	14	15	16	17	18
19	20	21	22	23	24	25
26	27	28	29	30	31	

September

M	Tu	W	Th	F	Sa	Su
						1
2	3	4	5	6	7	8
9	10	11	12	13	14	15
16	17	18	19	20	21	22
23	24	25	26	27	28	29
30						

October

M	Tu	W	Th	F	Sa	Su
	1	2	3	4	5	6
7	8	9	10	11	12	13
14	15	16	17	18	19	20
21	22	23	24	25	26	27
28	29	30	31			

November

M	Tu	W	Th	F	Sa	Su
				1	2	3
4	5	6	7	8	9	10
11	12	13	14	15	16	17
18	19	20	21	22	23	24
25	26	27	28	29	30	

December

M	Tu	W	Th	F	Sa	Su
						1
2	3	4	5	6	7	8
9	10	11	12	13	14	15
16	17	18	19	20	21	22
23	24	25	26	27	28	29
30	31					

Wednesday Years Since 1753

1753 – 1799	1800 – 1899	1900 – 1999	2000 – 2099
1755	1800	1902	2003
1766	1806	1913	2014
1777	1817	1919	2025
1783	1823	1930	2031
1794	1834	1941	2042
	1845	1947	2053
	1851	1958	2059
	1862	1969	2070
	1873	1975	2081
	1879	1986	2087
	1890	1997	2098

It was a Wednesday year when on . . . .

2nd November 1755 Marie Antoinette was born.

21st November 1783 The first manned balloon flight took place over Paris.

20th March 1806 The foundation stone of Dartmoor Prison was laid.

12th October 1845 Elizabeth Fry, the English prison reformer, died.

1st May 1851 The Great Exhibition was opened in London at the Crystal Palace.

15th June 1919 Alcock and Brown completed the first non stop trans Atlantic flight.

18th February 1930 The planet Pluto was first recorded by Clyde Tombaugh at Flagstaff, Arizona.

15th August 1947 India and Pakistan became independent countries.

21st July 1969 Neil Armstrong became the first man to walk on the moon.

14th/23rd December 1986 Dick Rutan and Jeana Yeager flew around the world in the specially constructed aircraft Voyager without refuelling.

The Wednesday Year

January

M	Tu	W	Th	F	Sa	Su
		1	2	3	4	5
6	7	8	9	10	11	12
13	14	15	16	17	18	19
20	21	22	23	24	25	26
27	28	29	30	31		

February

M	Tu	W	Th	F	Sa	Su
					1	2
3	4	5	6	7	8	9
10	11	12	13	14	15	16
17	18	19	20	21	22	23
24	25	26	27	28		

March

M	Tu	W	Th	F	Sa	Su
					1	2
3	4	5	6	7	8	9
10	11	12	13	14	15	16
17	18	19	20	21	22	23
24	25	26	27	28	29	30
31						

April

M	Tu	W	Th	F	Sa	Su
	1	2	3	4	5	6
7	8	9	10	11	12	13
14	15	16	17	18	19	20
21	22	23	24	25	26	27
28	29	30				

May

M	Tu	W	Th	F	Sa	Su
			1	2	3	4
5	6	7	8	9	10	11
12	13	14	15	16	17	18
19	20	21	22	23	24	25
26	27	28	29	30	31	

June

M	Tu	W	Th	F	Sa	Su
						1
2	3	4	5	6	7	8
9	10	11	12	13	14	15
16	17	18	19	20	21	22
23	24	25	26	27	28	29
30						

July

M	Tu	W	Th	F	Sa	Su
	1	2	3	4	5	6
7	8	9	10	11	12	13
14	15	16	17	18	19	20
21	22	23	24	25	26	27
28	29	30	31			

August

M	Tu	W	Th	F	Sa	Su
				1	2	3
4	5	6	7	8	9	10
11	12	13	14	15	16	17
18	19	20	21	22	23	24
25	26	27	28	29	30	31

September

M	Tu	W	Th	F	Sa	Su
1	2	3	4	5	6	7
8	9	10	11	12	13	14
15	16	17	18	19	20	21
22	23	24	25	26	27	28
29	30					

October

M	Tu	W	Th	F	Sa	Su
		1	2	3	4	5
6	7	8	9	10	11	12
13	14	15	16	17	18	19
20	21	22	23	24	25	26
27	28	29	30	31		

November

M	Tu	W	Th	F	Sa	Su
					1	2
3	4	5	6	7	8	9
10	11	12	13	14	15	16
17	18	19	20	21	22	23
24	25	26	27	28	29	30

December

M	Tu	W	Th	F	Sa	Su
1	2	3	4	5	6	7
8	9	10	11	12	13	14
15	16	17	18	19	20	21
22	23	24	25	26	27	28
29	30	31				

Thursday Years Since 1753

1753–1799	1800–1899	1900–1999	2000–2099
1761	1801	1903	2009
1767	1807	1914	2015
1778	1818	1925	2026
1789	1829	1931	2037
1795	1835	1942	2043
	1846	1953	2054
	1857	1959	2065
	1863	1970	2071
	1874	1981	2082
	1885	1987	2093
	1891	1998	2099

It was a Thursday year when on . . . .

14th July 1789 The Bastille was stormed during the French Revolution.

4th July 1829 The first London bus ran.

22nd February 1857 Lord Baden Powell, the founder of the Scout movement, was born.

7th November 1885 The Canadian Pacific Railroad was completed.

4th August 1914 Britain declared war on Germany thus entering the first world war.

13th October 1925 Margaret Thatcher, the British Prime Minister, was born.

29th May 1953 Edmund Hilary and Sherpa Tenzing became the first men to climb Mount Everest.

19th December 1959 Walter Williams, the last survivor of the American Civil War, died aged 117.

12th January 1970 The first jumbo jet, a Pan American Boeing 747, arrived at Heathrow Airport, London.

16th October 1987 The South and East of England was struck by a Great Storm.

The Thursday Year

January
M	Tu	W	Th	F	Sa	Su
			1	2	3	4
5	6	7	8	9	10	11
12	13	14	15	16	17	18
19	20	21	22	23	24	25
26	27	28	29	30	31	

February
M	Tu	W	Th	F	Sa	Su
						1
2	3	4	5	6	7	8
9	10	11	12	13	14	15
16	17	18	19	20	21	22
23	24	25	26	27	28	

March
M	Tu	W	Th	F	Sa	Su
						1
2	3	4	5	6	7	8
9	10	11	12	13	14	15
16	17	18	19	20	21	22
23	24	25	26	27	28	29
30	31					

April
M	Tu	W	Th	F	Sa	Su
	1	2	3	4	5	
6	7	8	9	10	11	12
13	14	15	16	17	18	19
20	21	22	23	24	25	26
27	28	29	30			

May
M	Tu	W	Th	F	Sa	Su
				1	2	3
4	5	6	7	8	9	10
11	12	13	14	15	16	17
18	19	20	21	22	23	24
25	26	27	28	29	30	31

June
M	Tu	W	Th	F	Sa	Su
1	2	3	4	5	6	7
8	9	10	11	12	13	14
15	16	17	18	19	20	21
22	23	24	25	26	27	28
29	30					

July
M	Tu	W	Th	F	Sa	Su
		1	2	3	4	5
6	7	8	9	10	11	12
13	14	15	16	17	18	19
20	21	22	23	24	25	26
27	28	29	30	31		

August
M	Tu	W	Th	F	Sa	Su
					1	2
3	4	5	6	7	8	9
10	11	12	13	14	15	16
17	18	19	20	21	22	23
24	25	26	27	28	29	30
31						

September
M	Tu	W	Th	F	Sa	Su
	1	2	3	4	5	6
7	8	9	10	11	12	13
14	15	16	17	18	19	20
21	22	23	24	25	26	27
28	29	30				

October
M	Tu	W	Th	F	Sa	Su
			1	2	3	4
5	6	7	8	9	10	11
12	13	14	15	16	17	18
19	20	21	22	23	24	25
26	27	28	29	30	31	

November
M	Tu	W	Th	F	Sa	Su
						1
2	3	4	5	6	7	8
9	10	11	12	13	14	15
16	17	18	19	20	21	22
23	24	25	26	27	28	29
30						

December
M	Tu	W	Th	F	Sa	Su
	1	2	3	4	5	6
7	8	9	10	11	12	13
14	15	16	17	18	19	20
21	22	23	24	25	26	27
28	29	30	31			

Friday Years Since 1753

1753 – 1799	1800 – 1899	1900 – 1999	2000 – 2099
1762	1802	1909	2010
1773	1813	1915	2021
1779	1819	1926	2027
1790	1830	1937	2038
	1841	1943	2049
	1847	1954	2055
	1858	1965	2066
	1869	1971	2077
	1875	1982	2083
	1886	1993	2094
	1897	1999	

It was a Friday year when on . . . .

14th February 1779 Captain James Cook, the explorer, was murdered.
5th March 1790 Flora Macdonald, who helped Bonnie Prince Charlie escape from Scotland, died.
15th September 1830 The Manchester to Liverpool Railway was opened.
17th November 1869 The first passage of ships through the Suez Canal was made.
25th August 1875 Captain Matthew Webb became the first man to swim the English Channel, without a life jacket.
6th April 1909 Two Americans Robert Peary and Matthew Hanson and four Eskimos Ooqueah, Egingwah, Seegloo and Ootah became the first men to reach the North Pole.
27th January 1926 John Logie Baird gave the first demonstration of television.
27th May 1937 The Golden Gate Bridge across San Francisco Bay was officially opened.
17th July 1954 Disneyland opened.
15th February 1971 The changeover to decimal currency was made in the United Kingdom.

The Friday Year

January

M	Tu	W	Th	F	Sa	Su
				1	2	3
4	5	6	7	8	9	10
11	12	13	14	15	16	17
18	19	20	21	22	23	24
25	26	27	28	29	30	31

February

M	Tu	W	Th	F	Sa	Su
1	2	3	4	5	6	7
8	9	10	11	12	13	14
15	16	17	18	19	20	21
22	23	24	25	26	27	28

March

M	Tu	W	Th	F	Sa	Su
1	2	3	4	5	6	7
8	9	10	11	12	13	14
15	16	17	18	19	20	21
22	23	24	25	26	27	28
29	30	31				

April

M	Tu	W	Th	F	Sa	Su
				1	2	3
5	6	7	8	9	10	11
12	13	14	15	16	17	18
19	20	21	22	23	24	25
26	27	28	29	30		

May

M	Tu	W	Th	F	Sa	Su
					1	2
3	4	5	6	7	8	9
10	11	12	13	14	15	16
17	18	19	20	21	22	23
24	25	26	27	28	29	30
31						

June

M	Tu	W	Th	F	Sa	Su
	1	2	3	4	5	6
7	8	9	10	11	12	13
14	15	16	17	18	19	20
21	22	23	24	25	26	27
28	29	30				

July

M	Tu	W	Th	F	Sa	Su
			1	2	3	4
5	6	7	8	9	10	11
12	13	14	15	16	17	18
19	20	21	22	23	24	25
26	27	28	29	30	31	

August

M	Tu	W	Th	F	Sa	Su
						1
2	3	4	5	6	7	8
9	10	11	12	13	14	15
16	17	18	19	20	21	22
23	24	25	26	27	28	29
30	31					

September

M	Tu	W	Th	F	Sa	Su
		1	2	3	4	5
6	7	8	9	10	11	12
13	14	15	16	17	18	19
20	21	22	23	24	25	26
27	28	29	30			

October

M	Tu	W	Th	F	Sa	Su
				1	2	3
4	5	6	7	8	9	10
11	12	13	14	15	16	17
18	19	20	21	22	23	24
25	26	27	28	29	30	31

November

M	Tu	W	Th	F	Sa	Su
1	2	3	4	5	6	7
8	9	10	11	12	13	14
15	16	17	18	19	20	21
22	23	24	25	26	27	28
29	30					

December

M	Tu	W	Th	F	Sa	Su
		1	2	3	4	5
6	7	8	9	10	11	12
13	14	15	16	17	18	19
20	21	22	23	24	25	26
27	28	29	30	31		

F

Saturday Years Since 1753

1753 – 1799	1800 – 1899	1900 – 1999	2000 – 2099
1757	1803	1910	2005
1763	1814	1921	2011
1774	1825	1927	2022
1785	1831	1938	2033
1791	1842	1949	2039
	1853	1955	2050
	1859	1966	2061
	1870	1977	2067
	1881	1983	2078
	1887	1994	2089
	1898		2095

It was a Saturday year when on . . . .

28th October 1831 Michael Faraday made the first dynamo.
30th June 1859 Blondin crossed the Niagara Falls on a tightrope with a man on his back.
27th June 1898 Joshua Slocum became the first man to sail single handed round the world.
4th June 1910 Christopher Cockerell, the inventor of the hovercraft, was born.
12th July 1910 Charles Stewart Rolls, the aviator and automobile manufacturer, was killed.
24th May 1927 Charles Lindbergh completed the first solo trans Atlantic flight.
19th October 1949 The Peoples Republic of China was proclaimed.
18th April 1955 Albert Einstein, the German mathematician, died.
27th July 1966 Brenda Sherrat became the first person to swim the length of Loch Ness (22¾ miles), Britain's longest lake.
16th August 1977 Elvis Presley, pop star, died.

The Saturday Year

January
M	Tu	W	Th	F	Sa	Su
					1	2
3	4	5	6	7	8	9
10	11	12	13	14	15	16
17	18	19	20	21	22	23
24	25	26	27	28	29	30
31						

February
M	Tu	W	Th	F	Sa	Su
	1	2	3	4	5	6
7	8	9	10	11	12	13
14	15	16	17	18	19	20
21	22	23	24	25	26	27
28						

March
M	Tu	W	Th	F	Sa	Su
	1	2	3	4	5	6
7	8	9	10	11	12	13
14	15	16	17	18	19	20
21	22	23	24	25	26	27
28	29	30	31			

April
M	Tu	W	Th	F	Sa	Su
				1	2	3
4	5	6	7	8	9	10
11	12	13	14	15	16	17
18	19	20	21	22	23	24
25	26	27	28	29	30	

May
M	Tu	W	Th	F	Sa	Su
						1
2	3	4	5	6	7	8
9	10	11	12	13	14	15
16	17	18	19	20	21	22
23	24	25	26	27	28	29
30	31					

June
M	Tu	W	Th	F	Sa	Su
		1	2	3	4	5
6	7	8	9	10	11	12
13	14	15	16	17	18	19
20	21	22	23	24	25	26
27	28	29	30			

July
M	Tu	W	Th	F	Sa	Su
				1	2	3
4	5	6	7	8	9	10
11	12	13	14	15	16	17
18	19	20	21	22	23	24
25	26	27	28	29	30	31

August
M	Tu	W	Th	F	Sa	Su
1	2	3	4	5	6	7
8	9	10	11	12	13	14
15	16	17	18	19	20	21
22	23	24	25	26	27	28
29	30	31				

September
M	Tu	W	Th	F	Sa	Su
			1	2	3	4
5	6	7	8	9	10	11
12	13	14	15	16	17	18
19	20	21	22	23	24	25
26	27	28	29	30		

October
M	Tu	W	Th	F	Sa	Su
					1	2
3	4	5	6	7	8	9
10	11	12	13	14	15	16
17	18	19	20	21	22	23
24	25	26	27	28	29	30
31						

November
M	Tu	W	Th	F	Sa	Su
	1	2	3	4	5	6
7	8	9	10	11	12	13
14	15	16	17	18	19	20
21	22	23	24	25	26	27
28	29	30				

December
M	Tu	W	Th	F	Sa	Su
			1	2	3	4
5	6	7	8	9	10	11
12	13	14	15	16	17	18
19	20	21	22	23	24	25
26	27	28	29	30	31	

Sa

Sunday Years Since 1753

1753 – 1799	1800 – 1899	1900 – 1999	2000 – 2099
1758	1809	1905	2006
1769	1815	1911	2017
1775	1826	1922	2023
1786	1837	1933	2034
1797	1843	1939	2045
	1854	1950	2051
	1865	1961	2062
	1871	1967	2073
	1882	1978	2079
	1893	1989	2090
	1899	1995	

It was a Sunday year when on . . . .

15th August 1769 Napoleon Bonaparte was born.

17th June 1775 The battle of Bunker Hill, which began the American War of Independence, was fought.

17th August 1786 Davy Crocket, the American pioneer, was born.

18th June 1815 The battle of Waterloo was fought.

27th September 1826 The first passenger railway was opened between Stockton and Darlington.

25th October 1854 The charge of the Light Brigade took place at Balaclava.

10th October 1871 Henry Morton Stanley, the journalist, met David Livingstone, the explorer, at Ujiji in Africa.

14th December 1911 A party of Norwegians, led by Roald Amundsen, became the first men to reach the South Pole.

12th April 1961 Yuri Gagarin, a Russian cosmonaut, became the first man in space.

6th August 1978 Pope Paul VI died, and then his successor Pope John Paul died less than two months later.

The Sunday Year

January
M	Tu	W	Th	F	Sa	Su
						1
2	3	4	5	6	7	8
9	10	11	12	13	14	15
16	17	18	19	20	21	22
23	24	25	26	27	28	29
30	31					

February
M	Tu	W	Th	F	Sa	Su
				1	2	3	4	5
6	7	8	9	10	11	12
13	14	15	16	17	18	19
20	21	22	23	24	25	26
27	28					

March
M	Tu	W	Th	F	Sa	Su
		1	2	3	4	5
6	7	8	9	10	11	12
13	14	15	16	17	18	19
20	21	22	23	24	25	26
27	28	29	30	31		

April
M	Tu	W	Th	F	Sa	Su
					1	2
3	4	5	6	7	8	9
10	11	12	13	14	15	16
17	18	19	20	21	22	23
24	25	26	27	28	29	30

May
M	Tu	W	Th	F	Sa	Su
1	2	3	4	5	6	7
8	9	10	11	12	13	14
15	16	17	18	19	20	21
22	23	24	25	26	27	28
29	30	31				

June
M	Tu	W	Th	F	Sa	Su
			1	2	3	4
5	6	7	8	9	10	11
12	13	14	15	16	17	18
19	20	21	22	23	24	25
26	27	28	29	30		

July
M	Tu	W	Th	F	Sa	Su
					1	2
3	4	5	6	7	8	9
10	11	12	13	14	15	16
17	18	19	20	21	22	23
24	25	26	27	28	29	30
31						

August
M	Tu	W	Th	F	Sa	Su
1	2	3	4	5	6	
7	8	9	10	11	12	13
14	15	16	17	18	19	20
21	22	23	24	25	26	27
28	29	30	31			

September
M	Tu	W	Th	F	Sa	Su
			1	2	3	
4	5	6	7	8	9	10
11	12	13	14	15	16	17
18	19	20	21	22	23	24
25	26	27	28	29	30	

October
M	Tu	W	Th	F	Sa	Su
						1
2	3	4	5	6	7	8
9	10	11	12	13	14	15
16	17	18	19	20	21	22
23	24	25	26	27	28	29
30	31					

November
M	Tu	W	Th	F	Sa	Su
	1	2	3	4	5	
6	7	8	9	10	11	12
13	14	15	16	17	18	19
20	21	22	23	24	25	26
27	28	29	30			

December
M	Tu	W	Th	F	Sa	Su
			1	2	3	
4	5	6	7	8	9	10
11	12	13	14	15	16	17
18	19	20	21	22	23	24
25	26	27	28	29	30	31

Su

Monday Leap Years Since 1753

1753 – 1799	1800 – 1899	1900 – 1999	2000 – 2099
1776	1816	1912	2024
	1844	1940	2052
	1872	1968	2080
		1996	

It was a Monday leap year when on . . . .

4th July 1776 The American Declaration of Independence was adopted.
21st April 1816 Charlotte Brontë, the author of Jane Eyre, was born.
1st July 1872 Louis Bleriot, the first man to fly across the English Channel, was born.
7th November 1872 The ship the Marie Celeste, later found abandoned, left New York.
14th/15th April 1912 The Titanic struck an iceberg and sank in the Atlantic Ocean.
23rd July 1940 The London blitz began with an all night German air raid.
31st December 1968 The highest Barometric pressure ever was recorded at Agata in Siberia.

The Monday Leap Year

January

M	Tu	W	Th	F	Sa	Su
1	2	3	4	5	6	7
8	9	10	11	12	13	14
15	16	17	18	19	20	21
22	23	24	25	26	27	28
29	30	31				

February

M	Tu	W	Th	F	Sa	Su
			1	2	3	4
5	6	7	8	9	10	11
12	13	14	15	16	17	18
19	20	21	22	23	24	25
26	27	28	29			

March

M	Tu	W	Th	F	Sa	Su
				1	2	3
4	5	6	7	8	9	10
11	12	13	14	15	16	17
18	19	20	21	22	23	24
25	26	27	28	29	30	31

April

M	Tu	W	Th	F	Sa	Su
1	2	3	4	5	6	7
8	9	10	11	12	13	14
15	16	17	18	19	20	21
22	23	24	25	26	27	28
29	30					

May

M	Tu	W	Th	F	Sa	Su
		1	2	3	4	5
6	7	8	9	10	11	12
13	14	15	16	17	18	19
20	21	22	23	24	25	26
27	28	29	30	31		

June

M	Tu	W	Th	F	Sa	Su
					1	2
3	4	5	6	7	8	9
10	11	12	13	14	15	16
17	18	19	20	21	22	23
24	25	26	27	28	29	30

July

M	Tu	W	Th	F	Sa	Su
1	2	3	4	5	6	7
8	9	10	11	12	13	14
15	16	17	18	19	20	21
22	23	24	25	26	27	28
29	30	31				

August

M	Tu	W	Th	F	Sa	Su
				1	2	3	4
5	6	7	8	9	10	11
12	13	14	15	16	17	18
19	20	21	22	23	24	25
26	27	28	29	30	31	

September

M	Tu	W	Th	F	Sa	Su
						1
2	3	4	5	6	7	8
9	10	11	12	13	14	15
16	17	18	19	20	21	22
23	24	25	26	27	28	29
30						

October

M	Tu	W	Th	F	Sa	Su
	1	2	3	4	5	6
7	8	9	10	11	12	13
14	15	16	17	18	19	20
21	22	23	24	25	26	27
28	29	30	31			

November

M	Tu	W	Th	F	Sa	Su
				1	2	3
4	5	6	7	8	9	10
11	12	13	14	15	16	17
18	19	20	21	22	23	24
25	26	27	28	29	30	

December

M	Tu	W	Th	F	Sa	Su
						1
2	3	4	5	6	7	8
9	10	11	12	13	14	15
16	17	18	19	20	21	22
23	24	25	26	27	28	29
30	31					

M

LEAP

Tuesday Leap Years Since 1753

1753 – 1799	1800 – 1899	1900 – 1999	2000 – 2099
1760	1828	1924	2008
1788	1856	1952	2036
	1884	1980	2064
			2092

It was a Tuesday leap year when on . . . .

5th February 1788 Sir Robert Peel, the British Prime Minister responsible for the introduction of the police force, was born.

8th November 1828 Thomas Bewick, the English wood engraver, died.

21st January 1856 The 350th anniversary of the formation of the Swiss guard at the Vatican City was celebrated.

13th March 1884 Standard time was adopted in the U.S.A.

2nd November 1924 The first crossword puzzle published in an English newspaper appeared in the Sunday Express.

6th February 1952 Queen Elizabeth $\overline{\text{II}}$ succeeded her father King George VI.

4th November 1980 Ronald Reagan was elected president of the U.S.A.

The Tuesday Leap Year

January

M	Tu	W	Th	F	Sa	Su
	1	2	3	4	5	6
7	8	9	10	11	12	13
14	15	16	17	18	19	20
21	22	23	24	25	26	27
28	29	30	31			

February

M	Tu	W	Th	F	Sa	Su
				1	2	3
4	5	6	7	8	9	10
11	12	13	14	15	16	17
18	19	20	21	22	23	24
25	26	27	28	29		

March

M	Tu	W	Th	F	Sa	Su
				1	2	
3	4	5	6	7	8	9
10	11	12	13	14	15	16
17	18	19	20	21	22	23
24	25	26	27	28	29	30
31						

April

M	Tu	W	Th	F	Sa	Su
	1	2	3	4	5	6
7	8	9	10	11	12	13
14	15	16	17	18	19	20
21	22	23	24	25	26	27
28	29	30				

May

M	Tu	W	Th	F	Sa	Su
			1	2	3	4
5	6	7	8	9	10	11
12	13	14	15	16	17	18
19	20	21	22	23	24	25
26	27	28	29	30	31	

June

M	Tu	W	Th	F	Sa	Su
						1
2	3	4	5	6	7	8
9	10	11	12	13	14	15
16	17	18	19	20	21	22
23	24	25	26	27	28	29
30						

July

M	Tu	W	Th	F	Sa	Su
	1	2	3	4	5	6
7	8	9	10	11	12	13
14	15	16	17	18	19	20
21	22	23	24	25	26	27
28	29	30	31			

August

M	Tu	W	Th	F	Sa	Su
				1	2	3
4	5	6	7	8	9	10
11	12	13	14	15	16	17
18	19	20	21	22	23	24
25	26	27	28	29	30	31

September

M	Tu	W	Th	F	Sa	Su
1	2	3	4	5	6	7
8	9	10	11	12	13	14
15	16	17	18	19	20	21
22	23	24	25	26	27	28
29	30					

October

M	Tu	W	Th	F	Sa	Su
		1	2	3	4	5
6	7	8	9	10	11	12
13	14	15	16	17	18	19
20	21	22	23	24	25	26
27	28	29	30	31		

November

M	Tu	W	Th	F	Sa	Su
					1	2
3	4	5	6	7	8	9
10	11	12	13	14	15	16
17	18	19	20	21	22	23
24	25	26	27	28	29	30

December

M	Tu	W	Th	F	Sa	Su
1	2	3	4	5	6	7
8	9	10	11	12	13	14
15	16	17	18	19	20	21
22	23	24	25	26	27	28
29	30	31				

Tu

LEAP

Wednesday Leap Years Since 1753

1753 – 1799	1800 – 1899	1900 – 1999	2000 – 2099
1772	1812	1908	2020
	1840	1936	2048
	1868	1964	2076
	1896	1992	

It was a Wednesday leap year when on . . . .

12th May 1812 Edward Lear, the poet and illustrator, was born.

19th October 1812 Napoleon began his retreat from Moscow.

1st October 1868 St Pancras Station in London was opened.

18th October 1896 The earliest strip cartoon, The Yellow Kid, appeared in the New York Times.

1st October 1908 Henry Ford introduced the model T motor car.

10th December 1936 King Edward VIII abdicated.

25th September 1964 Winston Churchill resigned as a member of Parliament after a period of service of nearly 64 years.

The Wednesday Leap Year

January

M	Tu	W	Th	F	Sa	Su
		1	2	3	4	5
6	7	8	9	10	11	12
13	14	15	16	17	18	19
20	21	22	23	24	25	26
27	28	29	30	31		

February

M	Tu	W	Th	F	Sa	Su
					1	2
3	4	5	6	7	8	9
10	11	12	13	14	15	16
17	18	19	20	21	22	23
24	25	26	27	28	29	

March

M	Tu	W	Th	F	Sa	Su
						1
2	3	4	5	6	7	8
9	10	11	12	13	14	15
16	17	18	19	20	21	22
23	24	25	26	27	28	29
30	31					

April

M	Tu	W	Th	F	Sa	Su
		1	2	3	4	5
6	7	8	9	10	11	12
13	14	15	16	17	18	19
20	21	22	23	24	25	26
27	28	29	30			

May

M	Tu	W	Th	F	Sa	Su
				1	2	3
4	5	6	7	8	9	10
11	12	13	14	15	16	17
18	19	20	21	22	23	24
25	26	27	28	29	30	31

June

M	Tu	W	Th	F	Sa	Su
1	2	3	4	5	6	7
8	9	10	11	12	13	14
15	16	17	18	19	20	21
22	23	24	25	26	27	28
29	30					

July

M	Tu	W	Th	F	Sa	Su
		1	2	3	4	5
6	7	8	9	10	11	12
13	14	15	16	17	18	19
20	21	22	23	24	25	26
27	28	29	30	31		

August

M	Tu	W	Th	F	Sa	Su
					1	2
3	4	5	6	7	8	9
10	11	12	13	14	15	16
17	18	19	20	21	22	23
24	25	26	27	28	29	30
31						

September

M	Tu	W	Th	F	Sa	Su
1	2	3	4	5	6	
7	8	9	10	11	12	13
14	15	16	17	18	19	20
21	22	23	24	25	26	27
28	29	30				

October

M	Tu	W	Th	F	Sa	Su
		1	2	3	4	
5	6	7	8	9	10	11
12	13	14	15	16	17	18
19	20	21	22	23	24	25
26	27	28	29	30	31	

November

M	Tu	W	Th	F	Sa	Su
						1
2	3	4	5	6	7	8
9	10	11	12	13	14	15
16	17	18	19	20	21	22
23	24	25	26	27	28	29
30						

December

M	Tu	W	Th	F	Sa	Su
1	2	3	4	5	6	
7	8	9	10	11	12	13
14	15	16	17	18	19	20
21	22	23	24	25	26	27
28	29	30	31			

LEAP

39

Thursday Leap Years Since 1753

1753–1799	1800–1899	1900–1999	2000–2099
1756	1824	1920	2004
1784	1852	1948	2032
	1880	1976	2060
			2088

It was a Thursday leap year when on . . . .

27th January 1756 Wolfgang Amadeus Mozart, the German composer, was born.

15th March 1852 Augusta Gregory, playwright and founder of the Abbey theatre in Dublin, was born.

4th March 1880 The Forth Bridge was opened.

11th November 1920 The body of the Unknown Soldier, commemorating all the soldiers who were killed in the first world war, was buried in Westminster Abbey in London.

30th January 1948 Mahatma Gandhi, the Indian patriot, was assassinated.

12th October 1948 The first Morris Minor car was produced.

4th December 1976 Benjamin Britten, the English composer, died.

The Thursday Leap Year

January
M	Tu	W	Th	F	Sa	Su
				1	2	3	4
5	6	7	8	9	10	11
12	13	14	15	16	17	18
19	20	21	22	23	24	25
26	27	28	29	30	31	

February
M	Tu	W	Th	F	Sa	Su
						1
2	3	4	5	6	7	8
9	10	11	12	13	14	15
16	17	18	19	20	21	22
23	24	25	26	27	28	29

March
M	Tu	W	Th	F	Sa	Su
1	2	3	4	5	6	7
8	9	10	11	12	13	14
15	16	17	18	19	20	21
22	23	24	25	26	27	28
29	30	31				

April
M	Tu	W	Th	F	Sa	Su
				1	2	3	4
5	6	7	8	9	10	11
12	13	14	15	16	17	18
19	20	21	22	23	24	25
26	27	28	29	30		

May
M	Tu	W	Th	F	Sa	Su
					1	2
3	4	5	6	7	8	9
10	11	12	13	14	15	16
17	18	19	20	21	22	23
24	25	26	27	28	29	30
31						

June
M	Tu	W	Th	F	Sa	Su
	1	2	3	4	5	6
7	8	9	10	11	12	13
14	15	16	17	18	19	20
21	22	23	24	25	26	27
28	29	30				

July
M	Tu	W	Th	F	Sa	Su
			1	2	3	4
5	6	7	8	9	10	11
12	13	14	15	16	17	18
19	20	21	22	23	24	25
26	27	28	29	30	31	

August
M	Tu	W	Th	F	Sa	Su
						1
2	3	4	5	6	7	8
9	10	11	12	13	14	15
16	17	18	19	20	21	22
23	24	25	26	27	28	29
30	31					

September
M	Tu	W	Th	F	Sa	Su
	1	2	3	4	5
6	7	8	9	10	11	12
13	14	15	16	17	18	19
20	21	22	23	24	25	26
27	28	29	30			

October
M	Tu	W	Th	F	Sa	Su
				1	2	3
4	5	6	7	8	9	10
11	12	13	14	15	16	17
18	19	20	21	22	23	24
25	26	27	28	29	30	31

November
M	Tu	W	Th	F	Sa	Su
1	2	3	4	5	6	7
8	9	10	11	12	13	14
15	16	17	18	19	20	21
22	23	24	25	26	27	28
29	30					

December
M	Tu	W	Th	F	Sa	Su
	1	2	3	4	5
6	7	8	9	10	11	12
13	14	15	16	17	18	19
20	21	22	23	24	25	26
27	28	29	30	31		

LEAP

Friday Leap Years Since 1753

1753 – 1799	1800 – 1899	1900 – 1999	2000 – 2099
1768	1808	1904	2016
1796	1836	1932	2044
	1864	1960	2072
	1892	1988	

It was a Friday leap year when on . . . .

6th November 1796 Catherine the Great, Empress of Russia, died.
27th December 1836 8 people were killed in an avalanche of snow at Lewes in Sussex.
4th July 1904 The construction of the Panama canal began.
19th March 1932 Sydney Harbour Bridge was officially opened.
10th May 1960 U.S.S. Triton became the first submarine to circumnavigate the globe.
8th November 1960 John F. Kennedy was elected President of the U.S.A.
8th November 1988 George Bush was elected President of the U.S.A.

The Friday Leap Year

January
M	Tu	W	Th	F	Sa	Su
				1	2	3
4	5	6	7	8	9	10
11	12	13	14	15	16	17
18	19	20	21	22	23	24
25	26	27	28	29	30	31

February
M	Tu	W	Th	F	Sa	Su
1	2	3	4	5	6	7
8	9	10	11	12	13	14
15	16	17	18	19	20	21
22	23	24	25	26	27	28
29						

March
M	Tu	W	Th	F	Sa	Su
	1	2	3	4	5	6
7	8	9	10	11	12	13
14	15	16	17	18	19	20
21	22	23	24	25	26	27
28	29	30	31			

April
M	Tu	W	Th	F	Sa	Su
				1	2	3
4	5	6	7	8	9	10
11	12	13	14	15	16	17
18	19	20	21	22	23	24
25	26	27	28	29	30	

May
M	Tu	W	Th	F	Sa	Su
						1
2	3	4	5	6	7	8
9	10	11	12	13	14	15
16	17	18	19	20	21	22
23	24	25	26	27	28	29
30	31					

June
M	Tu	W	Th	F	Sa	Su
		1	2	3	4	5
6	7	8	9	10	11	12
13	14	15	16	17	18	19
20	21	22	23	24	25	26
27	28	29	30			

July
M	Tu	W	Th	F	Sa	Su
				1	2	3
4	5	6	7	8	9	10
11	12	13	14	15	16	17
18	19	20	21	22	23	24
25	26	27	28	29	30	31

August
M	Tu	W	Th	F	Sa	Su
1	2	3	4	5	6	7
8	9	10	11	12	13	14
15	16	17	18	19	20	21
22	23	24	25	26	27	28
29	30	31				

September
M	Tu	W	Th	F	Sa	Su
			1	2	3	4
5	6	7	8	9	10	11
12	13	14	15	16	17	18
19	20	21	22	23	24	25
26	27	28	29	30		

October
M	Tu	W	Th	F	Sa	Su
					1	2
3	4	5	6	7	8	9
10	11	12	13	14	15	16
17	18	19	20	21	22	23
24	25	26	27	28	29	30
31						

November
M	Tu	W	Th	F	Sa	Su
	1	2	3	4	5	6
7	8	9	10	11	12	13
14	15	16	17	18	19	20
21	22	23	24	25	26	27
28	29	30				

December
M	Tu	W	Th	F	Sa	Su
			1	2	3	4
5	6	7	8	9	10	11
12	13	14	15	16	17	18
19	20	21	22	23	24	25
26	27	28	29	30	31	

F

LEAP

Saturday Leap Years Since 1753

1753 – 1799	1800 – 1899	1900 – 1999	2000 – 2099
1780	1820	1916	2000
	1848	1944	2028
	1876	1972	2056
			2084

It was a Saturday leap year when on . . . .

12th May 1820 Florence Nightingale, the pioneering English nurse, was born.
24th January 1848 Gold was first discovered in California.
7th March 1876 Alexander Graham Bell patented the first telephone.
22nd April 1916 Yehudi Menuhin, the violinist, was born.
17th September 1944 Reinhold Messner, the first man to climb the 14 mountains in the world over 8000m., was born.
21st December 1944 The Stanedge Canal Tunnel (the longest in England) was closed.
24th May 1972 'Spaghetti Junction' was opened on the M6 at Gravelly Hill outside Birmingham.

The Saturday Leap Year

January

M	Tu	W	Th	F	Sa	Su
					1	2
3	4	5	6	7	8	9
10	11	12	13	14	15	16
17	18	19	20	21	22	23
24	25	26	27	28	29	30
31						

February

M	Tu	W	Th	F	Sa	Su
	1	2	3	4	5	6
7	8	9	10	11	12	13
14	15	16	17	18	19	20
21	22	23	24	25	26	27
28	29					

March

M	Tu	W	Th	F	Sa	Su
	1	2	3	4	5	
6	7	8	9	10	11	12
13	14	15	16	17	18	19
20	21	22	23	24	25	26
27	28	29	30	31		

April

M	Tu	W	Th	F	Sa	Su
					1	2
3	4	5	6	7	8	9
10	11	12	13	14	15	16
17	18	19	20	21	22	23
24	25	26	27	28	29	30

May

M	Tu	W	Th	F	Sa	Su
1	2	3	4	5	6	7
8	9	10	11	12	13	14
15	16	17	18	19	20	21
22	23	24	25	26	27	28
29	30	31				

June

M	Tu	W	Th	F	Sa	Su
		1	2	3	4	
5	6	7	8	9	10	11
12	13	14	15	16	17	18
19	20	21	22	23	24	25
26	27	28	29	30		

July

M	Tu	W	Th	F	Sa	Su
				1	2	
3	4	5	6	7	8	9
10	11	12	13	14	15	16
17	18	19	20	21	22	23
24	25	26	27	28	29	30
31						

August

M	Tu	W	Th	F	Sa	Su
	1	2	3	4	5	6
7	8	9	10	11	12	13
14	15	16	17	18	19	20
21	22	23	24	25	26	27
28	29	30	31			

September

M	Tu	W	Th	F	Sa	Su
				1	2	3
4	5	6	7	8	9	10
11	12	13	14	15	16	17
18	19	20	21	22	23	24
25	26	27	28	29	30	

October

M	Tu	W	Th	F	Sa	Su
					1	
2	3	4	5	6	7	8
9	10	11	12	13	14	15
16	17	18	19	20	21	22
23	24	25	26	27	28	29
30	31					

November

M	Tu	W	Th	F	Sa	Su
	1	2	3	4	5	
6	7	8	9	10	11	12
13	14	15	16	17	18	19
20	21	22	23	24	25	26
27	28	29	30			

December

M	Tu	W	Th	F	Sa	Su
			1	2	3	
4	5	6	7	8	9	10
11	12	13	14	15	16	17
18	19	20	21	22	23	24
25	26	27	28	29	30	31

Sa

LEAP

45

Sunday Leap Years Since 1753

1753–1799	1800–1899	1900–1999	2000–2099
1764	1804	1928	2012
1792	1832	1956	2040
	1860	1984	2068
	1888		2096

It was a Sunday leap year when on . . . .

27th January 1832 Lewis Carroll, the author of Alice in Wonderland, was born.
3rd April 1860 The first Pony Express set out across America.
23rd July 1888 John Boyd Dunlop applied to patent the Pneumatic tyre.
18th June 1928 Amelia Earhart became the first woman to fly across the Atlantic.
20th December 1928 Harry Ramsden's fish and chip shop, now the largest in the world, opened in West Yorkshire.
3rd June 1956 Third Class Railway travel was abolished in Britain.
9th July 1984 York Minster was struck by lightning.